Song for the Slug

Edited by Jill Bennett

Sorry for the Slug

A COLLECTION OF GARDEN POETRY

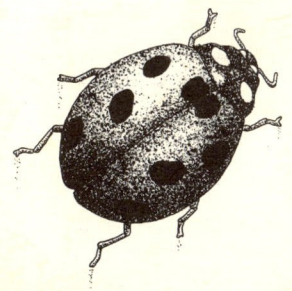

Illustrated by Alan Baker

MAMMOTH

Also by Jill Bennett
Spooky Poems
Tiny Tim, Verses for Children

This anthology first published in Great Britain 1994
by William Heinemann Ltd
Published 1995 by Mammoth
an imprint of Reed Consumer Books Ltd
Michelin House, 81 Fulham Road, London SW3 6RB
and Auckland, Melbourne, Singapore and Toronto

Copyright for this anthology © 1994 Jill Bennett
Illustrations copyright © 1994 Alan Baker

ISBN 0 7497 2334 3

A CIP catalogue record for this title
is available from the British Library

Printed and bound in Great Britain
by Cox & Wyman Ltd, Reading, Berkshire

This paperback is sold subject to the condition
that it shall not, by way of trade or otherwise,
be lent, resold, hired out, or otherwise circulated
without the publisher's prior consent in any form
of binding or cover other than that in which
it is published and without a similar condition
including this condition being imposed
on the subsequent purchaser.

Contents

Out and About *Shirley Hughes*	9
Snowdrop Poems *Sue Cowling*	10
Spring Sunshine *Tony Mitton*	11
Me First! *Beverly McLoughland*	12
Early Bird *Judith Nicholls*	13
Dandelions Everywhere *Aileen Fisher*	14
A Spike of Green *Barbara Baker*	15
The Digging Song *Wes Magee*	16
The Sun *Grace Nichols*	18
Lemon Moon *Beverly McLoughland*	19
There's a Murmur *Tony Bradman*	20
The Grass House *Shirley Hughes*	23

A Dragonfly *Eleanor Farjeon*	24
Firefly *Beverly McLoughland*	25
Slugs *John Kitching*	26
I Feel Sorry for the Slug *Judith Nicholls*	27
Ladybird Ladybird *John Agard*	28
Beetle, Beetle *Gina Douthwaite*	29
Caterpillar *Mary Dawson*	30
The Butterfly *Stanley Cook*	31
Riddle *Judith Nicholls*	32
Midsummer Night Itch *N. M. Boedecker*	33
Mumbling Bees *Daphne Lister*	34
Woodlouse *Judith Nicholls*	35

Under a Stone *Anon*	36
Snails *Theresa Heine*	37
Hey, Squirrel *Beverly McLoughland*	38
The Robin *L. Alma Tadema*	39
Daylight Robbery *Cynthia Mitchell*	40
I thought . . . *John Foster*	41
Grandad's Cats *Robin Mellor*	42
Acorn Haiku *Kit Wright*	43
Weeping Willow in my Garden *Ian Serraillier*	44
Seeds *Hilda I. Rostron*	45
Winter's Coming *Gina Douthwaite*	46
Winter *Theresa Heine*	47

That Noise Out There? *Sue Cowling*	48
If I Could Only . . . *John Agard*	49
Come on into my Tropical Garden *Grace Nichols*	50
Riddle *Grace Nichols*	51
Owl *Jean Kenward*	52
The Owl *Ruskin Bond*	54
Touch Wood *Pat Moon*	55
Hawthorn *Anne Bonner*	56
Raking Leaves *Ian Larmont*	58
The Trees *Ruskin Bond*	60

Out and About

Shiny boots,
Brand new,
Pale shoots
Poking through.
In the garden,
Out and about,
Run down the path,
Scamper and shout.
Wild white washing
Waves at the sky,
The birds are busy
And so am I.

SHIRLEY HUGHES

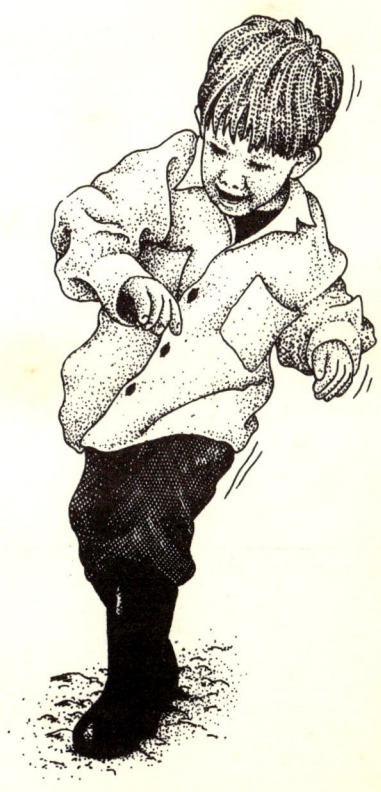

Snowdrop Poems

A flurry of snowdrops
a pale fire burning
a snowshower turning
to flower and flame

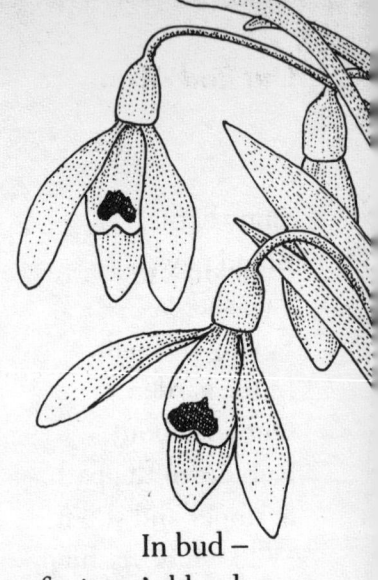

In bud –
a drop of winter's blood.
Awakening –
a bell to summon spring.

Pale blister
on the earth's hard gums
the snowdrop
spring's first milk-tooth
comes.

Snowdrop
hello!
little eskimo
bravo!

Slender stems
with gleaming hoods
fairy hairdryers
in the woods?

SUE COWLING

Spring Sunshine

Drenching the pavement,
warming the wall,
bathing the cat
in a slumbering sprawl

Shining the shell

on a beetle's back.
Feeding the weed
that springs from a crack.

Waking the buds
that break from the tree.
Shaking out gold,
and all for free.

TONY MITTON

Me First!

Yelp and swallow,
Swallow and yelp,
Ma and Pa Robin
Could use some help.

It's feed number one,
Number two, three, four;
It's me first, me first,
More, more, more!

It's whiz to the garden
Whiz to the tree;
It's me first, me first,
Me, me, me!

BEVERLY McLOUGHLAND

Early Bird

See how the blackbird
cocks his head;
'I'm listening for a worm!'
    he said.

JUDITH NICHOLLS

Dandelions Everywhere

The wind had some seeds
in his hand one day,
and he tripped on a bush
when he came our way.

He tripped on a bush
in our yard, he did,
and he dropped the seeds –
and they ran and hid.

They ran and hid
in the grass and clover
and didn't come out
till March was over.

And now that they're out
and we've more than our share
of dandelions
        dandelions
                everywhere.

AILEEN FISHER

A Spike of Green

When I went out
The sun was hot,
It shone upon
My flower pot.

And there I saw
A spike of green
That no-one else
Had ever seen!

On other days
The things I see
Are mostly old
Except for me.

But this green spike
So new and small
Had never yet
Been seen at all.

BARBARA BAKER

The Digging Song

In your hands you hold the spade.
Feel its well-worn wood,
Now you drive it in the earth.
Drive it deep and good.

   Dig dig digging dirt,
   Dirt inside your vest.
   Dig dig digging dirt,
   Digging dirt is best.

Here are worms that twist and loop
Tight as knots in string.
Here are spiders, ants and bugs
Running in a ring.

Dig dig digging dirt,
Dirt inside your vest.
Dig dig digging dirt,
Digging dirt is best.

Soon your hands are red and raw,
Blisters on the way.
But your spade just wants to dig
All the long, hot day.

Dig dig digging dirt,
Dirt inside your vest.
Dig dig digging dirt,
Digging dirt is best.

WES MAGEE

The Sun

The sun is a glowing spider
that crawls out
from under the earth
to make her way across the sky
warming and weaving
with her bright old fingers
of light.

GRACE NICHOLS

Lemon Moon

On a hot and thirsty summer night,
The moon's a wedge of lemon light
Sitting low among the trees,
Close enough for you to squeeze
And make a moonade, icy-sweet,
To cool your summer-dusty heat.

BEVERLY McLOUGHLAND

There's a Murmur

There's a murmur
In the garden
It's the sound
Of several bees
Humming there
And buzzing
Around our apple tree

There's a murmur
In the garden
It's the sound
Of granny's snores
She's lying
In a deckchair
(And she's showing
Us her drawers)

There's a murmur
In the garden
It's the bees
They're getting close
Getting near
Her mouth now . . .
One's landed
On her nose

There's a silence
In the garden
We're all waiting
Holding breath . . .
Will the bee
Sting granny?
We're all scared
To death . . .

There's a murmur
In the garden
It's the sound
Of one small bee
Leaving granny's
Snoring face
Settling on
Her knee

There's a murmur
In the garden
It's granny
Dreaming dreams
She's brushing
Bees off knees now . . .
It makes us
Want to scream!

There's a yawning
In the garden
And all the bees
Have gone . . .
Granny's waking
Up now —
'Have I been
Sleeping long?'

TONY BRADMAN

The Grass House

The grass house
Is my private place.
Nobody can see me
In the grass house.
Feathery plumes
Meet over my head.
Down here,
In the green, there are:
Seeds
Weeds
Stalks
Pods
And tiny little flowers.

Only the cat
And some busy, hurrying ants
Know where my grass house is.

SHIRLEY HUGHES

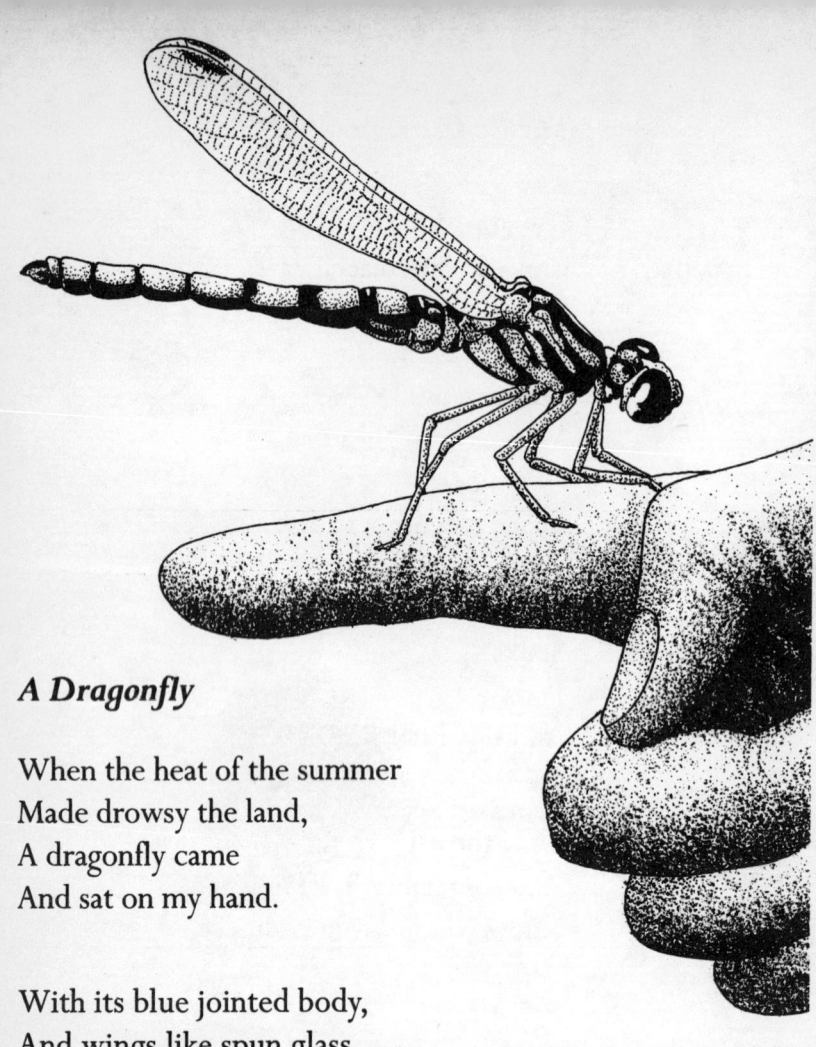

A Dragonfly

When the heat of the summer
Made drowsy the land,
A dragonfly came
And sat on my hand.

With its blue jointed body,
And wings like spun glass,
It lit on my fingers
As though they were grass.

ELEANOR FARJEON

Firefly

Cup your hands
Around a firefly –
In its cage of
Summer night

It will flicker
Through your fingers
Like a caught star –
Small and bright.

BEVERLY McLOUGHLAND

Slugs

Slugs, slugs
Crawl through the grass,
Watching all the beetles
As they scurry past.

Slugs, slugs
Crawl so slow,
Leaving tracks of silver
Wherever they go.

Slugs, slugs
Crawl along the wall
Popping little horns out
Make no sound at all.

JOHN KITCHING

I Feel Sorry For The Slug

He has to live on cabbage –
rather him than me!
I really wouldn't want to eat
just leaves AND leaves for tea!

(and leaves and leaves and leaves and leaves and
leaves . . .)

JUDITH NICHOLLS

Ladybird Ladybird

Ladybird
Ladybird

Have you heard
the birds
laughing?
They say you can't sing

But ladybird
I don't care
if you can't sing
I like how you move
your red and black wing.

JOHN AGARD

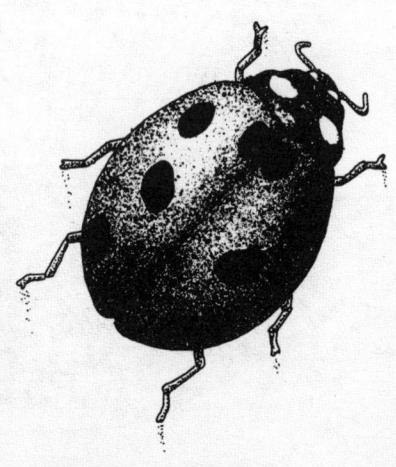

Beetle, Beetle

Beetle, beetle on your back

threads of legs a-rowing

from your saucered shell of black,

won't get where you're going

lest the ants can set you rolling

like a boat at sea,

tip you so your shell is showing

stick you back upon your feet.

GINA DOUTHWAITE

Caterpillar

Creepy crawly caterpillar
Looping up and down,
Furry tufts of hair along
Your back of golden brown.

You will soon be wrapped in silk,
Asleep for many a day;
And then, a handsome butterfly,
You'll stretch and fly away.

MARY DAWSON

The Butterfly

The sun is on fire
In the sky
And in its warmth
Flowers open
In the garden
And the butterfly
Flutters by.

        Wings widespread
        It stops to feed
        At the flowerbed
        And on its favourite flower
        The butterfly settles
        Like two extra petals.

STANLEY COOK

Riddle

I am . .
   spiral.
      Twisting shell
         on velvet black;
            track of silver,
               glider-one-foot,
                  home on back.
                     Leaf-feast hunter,
                      stalk-eyes high
                          above the leaf-feast trail.
                         What am I . . .?

                                     SNAIL!

JUDITH NICHOLLS

Midsummer Night Itch

Mosquito is out,
it's the end of the day;
she's humming and hunting
her evening away.

Who knows why such hunger
arrives on such wings
at sundown? I guess
it's the nature of things.

N.M. BOEDECKER

Mumbling Bees

All around the garden flowers
Big velvet bees are bumbling,
They hover low and as they go
They're mumbling, mumbling, mumbling.

To lavender and snapdragons
The busy bees keep coming,
And all the busy afternoon
They're humming, humming, humming.

Inside each bell-shaped flower and rose
They busily go stumbling,
Collecting pollen all day long
And bumbling, bumbling, bumbling.

DAPHNE LISTER

Woodlouse

Armoured dinosaur,
blundering through jungle grass by
dandelion-light.

Knight's headpiece, steel-hinged
orange-segment, ball-bearing,
armadillo-drop.

Pale peppercorn, pearled
eyeball; sentence without end,
my rolling full-stop.

JUDITH NICHOLLS

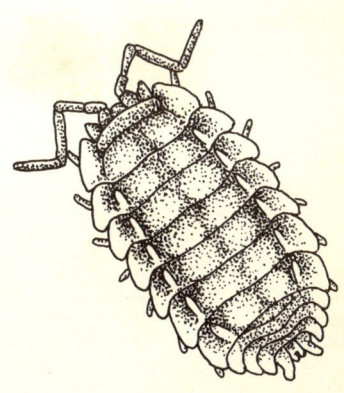

Under a Stone

Under a stone where the earth was firm,
I found a wriggly, wriggly worm;
'Good morning,' I said.
'How are you today?'
But the wriggly worm just wriggled away.

ANON.

Snails

Snails don't walk.
They slither and slide,
Along wet pathways
Gleam and glide,
Squeezed between
The grasses green,
Polished houses shell-like gleam.

THERESA HEINE

Hey, Squirrel

Hey, Squirrel,

What's the hurry?

Full of fear

And full of worry —

What's the hassle? What's the rush?

Acorns, beech nuts, seeds and such —

Food for young ones. Food for wife.

What's the frantic fuss for?

Life.

BEVERLY McLOUGHLAND

The Robin

When father takes his spade to dig,
    Then robin comes along;
He sits upon a little twig
    And sings a little song.

Or, if the trees are rather far,
    He does not stay alone,
But comes up close to where we are
    And bobs upon a stone.

L. ALMA TADEMA

Daylight Robbery

I'm weeding
And I'm seeding
In my vegetable patch,
And knowing
When I go in
That there's going to be a snatch.

That sparrow
On that barrow
And that robin on the gate
And those thrushes
In the bushes
Are all lying in wait.

CYNTHIA MITCHELL

I thought . . .

I thought it was
a hedgehog
but it was only
an old scrubbing brush
half-buried in the snow.

I thought it was
a blackbird
but it was only
some torn black plastic
caught in the branch of a tree.

I thought it was
a butterfly
but it was only
a scrap of paper
whirling about in the wind.

JOHN FOSTER

Grandad's Cats

Our garden is full of cats.

Some are all white, some all black,

There's a tabby that has long ears.

a big tom cat with ginger fur,

and, if you look, you'll find even more –

because Grandad puts food down by the door.

ROBIN MELLOR

Acorn Haiku

Just a green olive
In its own little egg-cup:
It can feed the sky.

KIT WRIGHT

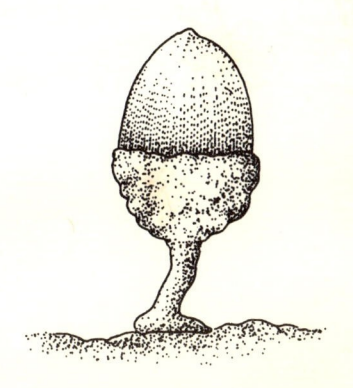

Weeping Willow in my Garden

My willow's like a frozen hill
Of green waves, when the wind is still;
But when it blows, the waves unfreeze
And makes a waterfall of leaves.

IAN SERRAILLIER

Seeds

Seeds that twist and seeds that twirl
Seeds with wings which spin and whirl;

Seeds that float on thistledown
Seeds in coats of glossy brown;

Seeds that burst with popping sound
From their pods to reach the ground;

Seeds with hooks that clutch and cling:
Seeds I plant for flowers next spring.

HILDA I. ROSTRON

Winter's Coming

Under a fringe of fidgeting leaves
stare round-ringed, wrinkled eyes
and under these a gnarled nose grows
and the old oak sighs

sighs from a hole at the foot of its bole
as its crisp crown quivers
Winter's coming to kiss goodnight.
The old oak *shivers*.

GINA DOUTHWAITE

Winter

Winter's sharp and spiky fingers
Grasping, freeze a world of ice,
Scattered snowflakes, soft as whispers,
Dream upon a quilt of white.

Grey and silver, world of winter,
Cold winds tell a frosted song,
Broken ice, like mirror splinters,
Forms across the frozen pond.

THERESA HEINE

That Noise Out There?

That noise out there?
It's the trees' knees knocking
with the cold.
They sold
their shirts
to the wind in the autumn,
now the winter's caught them
in their underwear!

SUE COWLING

If I Could Only

If I Could
Only Take
Home a
Snowflake

Snowflakes
like tiny
insects
drifting
down.

Snowflakes
like tiny
insects,
drifting
down.

Without a hum
they come,
without a hum
they go.

If only
I could take
one
home with me
to show
my friends
in the sun,
just for fun,
just for fun.

JOHN AGARD

Come on into my Tropical Garden

Come on into my tropical garden
Come on in and have a laugh in
Taste my sugar cake and my pine drink
Come on in please come on in

And yes you can stand up in my hammock
and breeze out in my trees
you can pick my hibiscus
And kiss my chimpanzees

O you can roll up in the grass
and if you pick up a flea
I'll take you down for a quick dip-wash
in the sea
believe me there's nothing better for getting rid of
a flea
than having a dip-wash in the sea

Come on into my tropical garden
Come on in please come on in.

GRACE NICHOLS

Riddle

Me-riddle me-riddle me-ree
Me father got a tree
Tell me what you see
hanging from this tree

You can boil it
you can bake it
you can roast it
you can fry it
it goes lovely in a dish
with flying fish

It's big
it's rough
it's green
it came with old Captain Bligh
from way across the sea

Still can't guess?
well it's a breadfruit
Me-riddle me-riddle me-ree.

GRACE NICHOLS

Owl

Wait here –
   will you wait here
under this tree?

Keep still –
   or, if you move,
move silently;

For
   as the darkness comes
an owl will fly

Out of
   the blackened sky.

Wait here –
   will you stay, too?
Often I stand

Watching
   the night creep up
over the land,

Till
   while the timid birds
make a todo

An owl
   comes flopping out
of the dark yew.

JEAN KENWARD

The Owl

At night, when all is still,
The forest's sentinel
Glides silently across the hill
And perches in an old pine tree.
A friendly presence his!
No harm can come
From night bird on the prowl.
His cry is mellow,
Much softer than a peacock's call.
When then this fear of owls
Calling in the night?
If men must speak
Then owls must hoot –
They have the right.
On me it casts no spell:
Rather, it seems to cry,
'The night is good – all's well, all's well.'

RUSKIN BOND

Touch Wood

Touch wood and feel her spirit move
   in the trembling of her leaves,

Touch wood and smell the perfume
   of the precious air she breathes,

Touch wood and taste the flavours
   of her fruits that we receive,

Touch wood and see against the sky
   the lace her fingers weave,

Touch wood and hear her branches conduct
   the rhythm of the breeze,

Touch wood that others take the time
   to listen to the trees.

PAT MOON

Hawthorn

A May tree is
a wonderful thing.
In late spring
its flowers, milky white
and scented with
the oncoming of night,
are tiny, perfect blooms
like many shining moons
on every branch.

In autumn when
the leaves turn gold
the tree is still
a wonder to behold.
Its blossoms have become
rosy red berries ripened
by the summer sun.
These are the haws
of the prickly tree.

Never harm the
hawthorn. Never cut
it down because
it is the magical
mysterious fairy tree.
It must grow unmolested.
It must grow free.

ANN BONNER

Raking Leaves

Raking leaves
Raking leaves
Raking raking leaves.

Heavy gloves
Long sleeves
Raking raking leaves.

Is that rain?
Not again!
Raking raking leaves.

Faster faster
Start to get
My t-shirt is soaked in sweat.

How is it
I'm always wet
Raking raking leaves?

IAN LARMONT

The Trees

At seven, when dusk slips over the mountains,
The trees start whispering among themselves.
They have been standing still all day,
But now they stretch their limbs in the dark,
Shifting a little, flexing their fingers,
Remembering the time when
They too walked the earth with men.
They know me well, these trees:
Oak and walnut, spruce and pine,
They know my face in the window,
They know me for a dreamer of dreams,
A world-loser, one of them.
They watch me while I watch them grow.
I listen to their whisperings,
Their own mysterious diction;
And bow my head before their arms
And ask for benediction.

RUSKIN BOND

Index of Poets

John Agard *Ladybird Ladybird*	28
If I Could Only . . .	49
Anon. *Under a Stone*	36
Barbara Baker *A Spike of Green*	15
N. M. Boedecker *Midsummer Night Itch*	33
Ruskin Bond *The Owls*	54
The Trees	60
Anne Bonner *Hawthorn*	56
Tony Bradman *There's a Murmur*	20
Stanley Cook *The Butterfly*	31
Sue Cowling *Snowdrop Poems*	10
That Noise Out There?	48
Mary Dawson *Caterpillar*	30
Gina Douthwaite *Beetle, Beetle*	29
Winter's Coming	46
Eleanor Farjeon *A Dragonfly*	24
Aileen Fisher *Dandelions Everywhere*	14
John Foster *I thought . . .*	41
Theresa Heine *Snails*	37
Winter	47
Shirley Hughes *The Grass House*	23
Out and About	9
Jean Kenward *Owl*	52
John Kitching *Slugs*	26
Ian Larmont *Raking Leaves*	58
Daphne Lister *Mumbling Bees*	34

Wes Magee *The Digging Song*	16
Beverly McLoughland *Firefly*	25
Hey, Squirrel	38
Lemon Moon	19
Me First!	12
Robin Mellor *Grandad's Cats*	42
Cynthia Mitchell *Daylight Robbery*	40
Tony Mitton *Spring Sunshine*	11
Pat Moon *Touch Wood*	55
Judith Nicholls *Early Bird*	13
I Feel Sorry for the Slug	27
Riddle	32
Woodlouse	35
Grace Nichols *Come on into my Tropical Garden*	50
The Sun	18
Riddle	51
Hilda I. Rostron *Seeds*	45
Ian Serraillier *Weeping Willow in my Garden*	44
L. Alma Tadema *The Robin*	39
Kit Wright *Acorn Haiku*	43

Acknowledgements

'Out and About' and 'The Grass House' by Shirley Hughes from *Out and About* (Walker Books 1988), copyright © Shirley Hughes 1988.
'Snowdrop Poems' and 'That Noise Out There?' by Sue Cowling, copyright © Sue Cowling 1994.
'Spring Sunshine' by Tony Mitton, copyright © Tony Mitton 1994.
'Me First!' by Beverly McLoughland from *Ranger Rick* magazine, April 1990 (National Wildlife Federation), © Beverly McLoughland 1990.
'Early Bird' by Judith Nicholls from *Jigglewords* (Thomas Nelson 1993), © Judith Nicholls 1993.
'Dandelions Everywhere' by Aileen Fisher from *Cricket in a Thicket* (Charles Scribner's Sons NY 1963), copyright © Aileen Fisher 1963.
'A Spike of Green' by Barbara Baker from *All Day Long* edited by Pamela Whitlock (Oxford University Press 1954), copyright © Barbara Baker 1954.
'The Digging Song' by Wes Magee from *The Witch's Brew and other Poems* compiled by Wes Magee (Cambridge University Press 1989), copyright © Wes Magee 1989.
'The Sun', 'Riddle' and 'Come on into my Tropical Garden by Grace Nichols from *Come on into my Tropical Garden* (A. & C. Black 1988), copyright © Grace Nichols 1988.
'Lemon Moon' by Beverly McLoughland from *Ranger Rick* magazine, November 1990 (National Wildlife Federation), copyright © Beverly McLoughland 1990.
'There's a Murmur' by Tony Bradman from *All Together Now* (Viking Children's Books 1989), copyright © Tony Bradman 1989.
'A Dragonfly' by Eleanor Farjeon from *Silver, Sand and Snow* (Michael Joseph 1951), copyright © Eleanor Farjeon 1951.
'Firefly' by Beverly McLoughland, copyright © Beverly McLoughland 1994.
'Slugs' by John Kitching from *Hi-Ran-Ho* compiled by N. & A. Chambers (Longman Young Books 1971), copyright © John Kitching 1971.
'I Feel Sorry for the Slug' by Judith Nicholls, copyright © Judith Nicholls 1994.
'Ladybird Ladybird' by John Agard from *No Hickory, No Dickory, No Dock* (Viking 1991), copyright © John Agard 1991.
'Beetle, Beetle' and 'Winter's Coming' by Gina Douthwaite, copyright © Gina Douthwaite 1994.

'Caterpillar' by Mary Dawson from *Sit on the Roofs and Holler*, coll. by Adrian Rumble (Puffin 1984), copyright © Mary Dawson 1984.
'The Butterfly' by Stanley Cook from *Another First Poetry Book* edited by J. Foster (Oxford University Press 1987), copyright © Stanley Cook 1987.
'Riddle' by Judith Nicholls from *Have You Ever?* (Mary Glasgow 1990), copyright © Judith Nicholls 1990.
'Midsummer Night Itch' by N. M. Boedecker from *Water Pennies* copyright © N. M. Boedecker.
'Mumbling Bees' by Daphne Lister, copyright © Daphne Lister 1994.
'Woodlouse' by Judith Nicholls from *Midnight Forest* (Faber & Faber 1985), copyright © Judith Nicholls 1985.
'Snails' and 'Winter' by Theresa Heine, copyright © Theresa Heine 1994.
'Hey, Squirrel' by Beverly McLoughland from *A Hippo's a Heap and other Animal Poems* by Beverly McLoughland (Boyds Mills Press 1993), copyright © Beverly McLoughland 1993.
'The Robin' by L. Alma Tadema from *Seeing and Doing* (Thames Methuen 1982).
'Daylight Robbery' by Cynthia Mitchell from *A Big Poetry Book* compiled by Wes Magee (Blackwell 1989), copyright © Cynthia Mitchell 1989.
'I thought...' by John Foster from *My Violet Poetry Book* edited by Moira Andrew (Macmillan Educational 1988), copyright © John Foster 1988.
'Grandad's Cats' by Robin Mellor, copyright © Robin Mellor 1994.
'Acorn Haiku' by Kit Wright from *Cat Among the Pigeons* (Viking 1984, Puffin 1987), copyright © Kit Wright 1984, 1987.
'Weeping Willow in my Garden' by Ian Serraillier from *I'll Tell You A Tale* (Longman Young Books 1973), copyright © Ian Serraillier 1973.
'Seeds' by Hilda I. Rostron from *Seeing and Doing* (Thames Methuen 1977), copyright © Hilda J. Rostron 1977.
'If I Could Only...' by John Agard from *I Din Do Nuttin'* (Bodley Head 1983), copyright © John Agard 1983.
'Owl' by Jean Kenward, copyright © Jean Kenward 1994.
'The Owl' and 'The Trees' by Ruskin Bond from *An Island of Trees* (Ratna Sagar Press Ltd, Delhi 1992), copyright © Ruskin Bond 1992.
'Touch Wood' by Pat Moon from *Earth Lines* (Pimlico Publishing 1991), copyright © Pat Moon 1991.
'Hawthorn' by Ann Bonner, copyright © Ann Bonner 1994.
'Raking Leaves' by Ian Larmont, © Ian Larmont.